Blastoff! Readers are carefully developed by literacy experts to build reading stamina and move students toward fluency by combining standards-based content with developmentally appropriate text.

Level 1 provides the most support through repetition of high-frequency words, light text, predictable sentence patterns, and strong visual support.

Level 2 offers early readers a bit more challenge through varied sentences, increased text load, and text-supportive special features.

Level 3 advances early-fluent readers toward fluency through increased text load, less reliance on photos, advancing concepts, longer sentences, and more complex special features.

★ **Blastoff! Universe**

This edition first published in 2024 by Bellwether Media, Inc.

No part of this publication may be reproduced in whole or in part without written permission of the publisher. For information regarding permission, write to Bellwether Media, Inc., Attention: Permissions Department, 6012 Blue Circle Drive, Minnetonka, MN 55343.

Library of Congress Cataloging-in-Publication Data

LC record for Indonesia available at: https://lccn.loc.gov/2023046594

Text copyright © 2024 by Bellwether Media, Inc. BLASTOFF! READERS and associated logos are trademarks and/or registered trademarks of Bellwether Media, Inc.

Editor: Rachael Barnes   Designer: Gabriel Hilger

Printed in the United States of America, North Mankato, MN.

Table of Contents

All About Indonesia	4
Land and Animals	6
Life in Indonesia	12
Indonesia Facts	20
Glossary	22
To Learn More	23
Index	24

All About Indonesia

Jakarta

Indonesia is an **archipelago**. Its islands spread across the Pacific and Indian Oceans.

Its capital was Jakarta until late 2024. Then, the capital moved to Nusantara.

Land and Animals

Indonesia's larger islands are lined with mountains. Many are **volcanoes**!

Rain forests surround the mountains. Some islands have **swamps** along the coasts.

rain forest

Mount Merapi

Size: 9,551 feet (2,911 meters) tall
Famous For: the most active volcano on the island of Java

broken building after an earthquake

Indonesia is often warm and rainy. It is cooler in the mountains. **Earthquakes** are common.

Monsoons occur between December and March. These winds bring lots of rain.

rain from a monsoon

Komodo dragons wait in the shade. They hunt deer. Tigers blend in with rain forest plants.

Sumatran tiger

Peafowl live near water. Males show off their bright feathers.

Life in Indonesia

More than half of Indonesians live on the island of Java. Most Indonesians are **Muslims**.

The official language is Bahasa Indonesia. Many people speak more than one language.

dance

puppet shadow play

Indonesia has many talented artists. They tell stories through dances and puppet shadow plays.

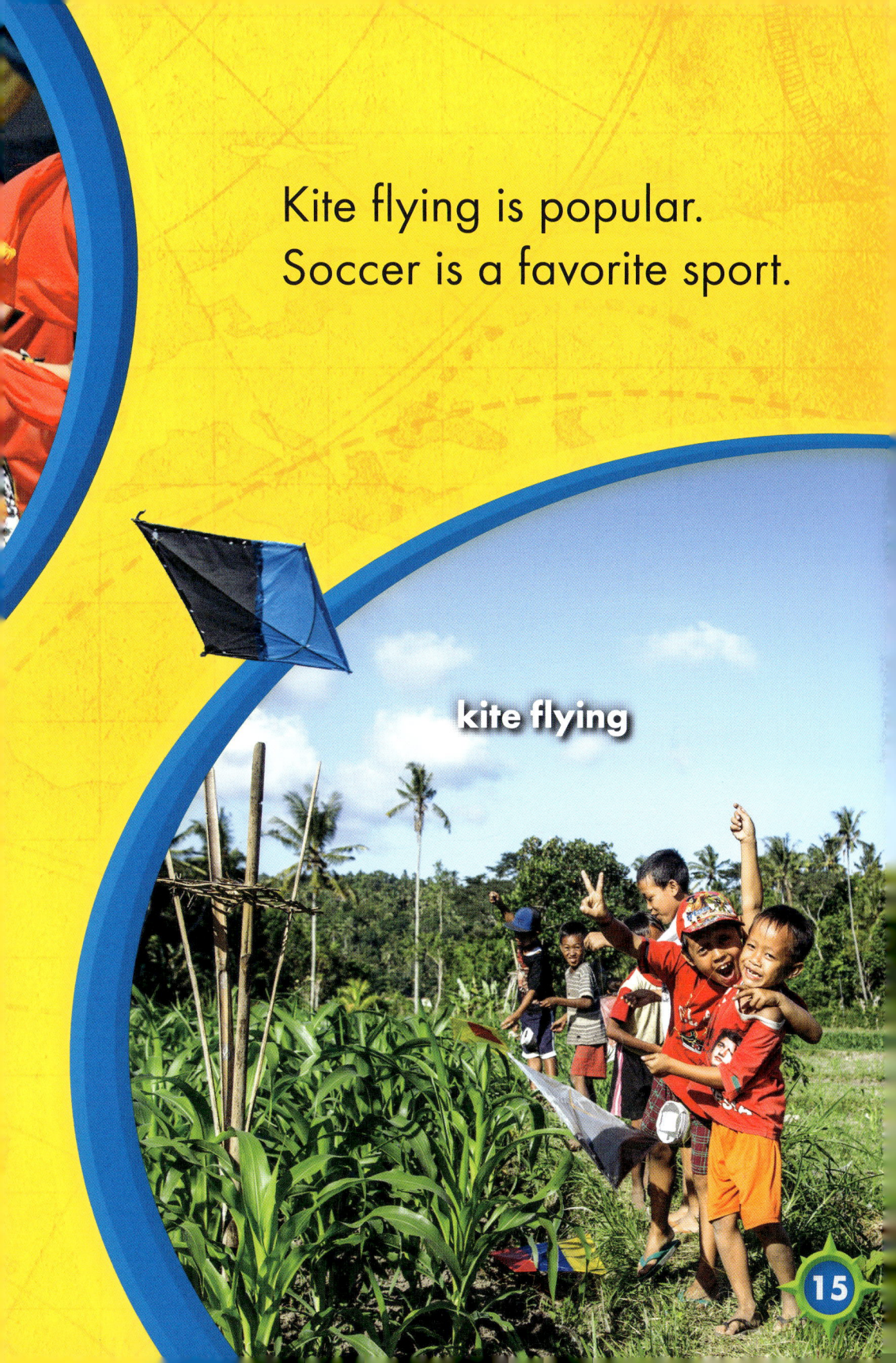

Kite flying is popular.
Soccer is a favorite sport.

kite flying

Gado-gado is a popular salad served with peanut sauce. Bakso is a vegetable and meatball soup.

Indonesian Foods

gado-gado

bakso

rice

klepon

bakso

Rice is eaten a lot. It is even used in *klepon* and other desserts!

Muslims **celebrate** Lebaran at the end of a month of **fasting**. They feast and pray with family.

Independence Day is August 17. People run races and play games!

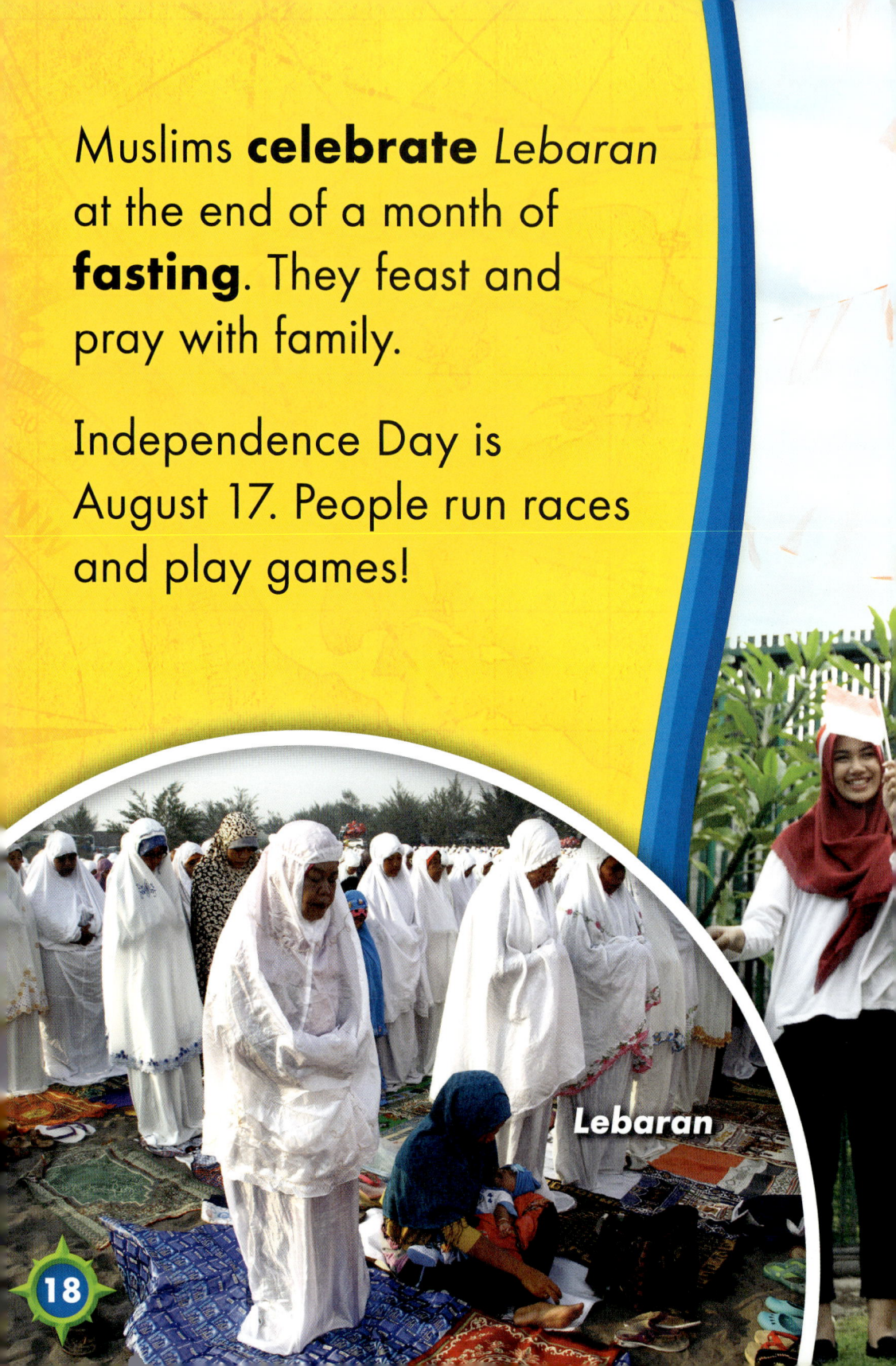

Lebaran

Independence Day

Indonesia Facts

Size:
735,358 square miles
(1,904,568 square kilometers)

Population:
279,476,346 (2023)

National Holiday:
Independence Day (August 17)

Main Language:
Bahasa Indonesia

Capital City:
Jakarta

Famous Face

Name: Agnes Monica Muljoto (known as Agnez Mo)
Famous For: international singer who speaks out against drug use

Religions

- Muslim 87%
- Christian 10%
- other: 1%
- Hindu 2%

Top Landmarks

Borobudur Temple

Kelimutu Crater Lakes

Komodo National Park

Glossary

archipelago—a group of islands

celebrate—to do something special or fun for an event, occasion, or holiday

earthquakes—sudden movements of the earth's crust

fasting—when you stop eating all or some foods for a certain period of time

monsoons—winds that shift direction each season; monsoons bring heavy rain.

Muslims—people of the Islamic faith; Muslims follow the teachings of Muhammad as told to him from Allah.

rain forests—thick, green forests that receive a lot of rain

swamps—areas of wet land that are filled with trees and other woody plants

volcanoes—holes in the earth; when a volcano erupts, hot ash, gas, and melted rock called lava shoots out.

To Learn More

AT THE LIBRARY
Murray, Julie. *Komodo Dragon*. Minneapolis, Minn.: ABDO, 2020.

Rose, Rachel. *Indonesia*. New York, N.Y.: Bearport Publishing Company, 2020.

Spanier, Kristine. *Indonesia*. Minneapolis, Minn.: Pogo Books, 2021.

ON THE WEB

FACTSURFER

Factsurfer.com gives you a safe, fun way to find more information.

1. Go to www.factsurfer.com.
2. Enter "Indonesia" into the search box and click 🔍.
3. Select your book cover to see a list of related content.

Index

animals, 10, 11
archipelago, 4
Bahasa Indonesia, 12, 13
capital (see Jakarta)
coasts, 6
dances, 14
earthquakes, 8
food, 16, 17
Independence Day, 18, 19
Indian Ocean, 4
Indonesia facts, 20–21
islands, 4, 6, 12
Jakarta, 4, 5
Java, 12
kite flying, 15
Lebaran, 18

map, 5
monsoons, 9
Mount Merapi, 7
mountains, 6, 7, 8
Muslims, 12, 18
Nusantara, 5
Pacific Ocean, 4
people, 12, 14, 18
puppet shadow plays, 14
rain, 8, 9
rain forests, 6, 10
say good day, 13
soccer, 15
swamps, 6
volcanoes, 6, 7

The images in this book are reproduced through the courtesy of: paha1205, front cover; Pav-Pro Photography Ltd, pp. 2-3; Bayu Putranto, p. 3 (flag); Creativa Images, pp. 4-5; menett, p. 6; Eugene Ga/ Alamy, pp. 6-7; R3 Livingworld, pp. 8-9; Maria_Usp, p. 9; blickwinkel/ Alamy, pp. 10-11; Sergey Uryadnikov, p. 11 (Komodo dragon); Erni 145612459, p. 11 (Timor deer); Upen supendi, p. 11 (Sumatran tiger); PUGUH YUDHA, p. 11 (green peafowl); Rachmad Darmawan, p. 12; Sony Herdiana, pp. 12-13; DODO HAWE, pp. 14-15 (dance); Aditia fidiantoro, p. 14 (puppet shadow play); Oliver Foerstner, p. 15 (kite flying); Hanifah Kurniati, p. 16 (*gado-gado*); Odua Images, pp. 16 (*bakso and klepon*), 17, 18-19; Rizkyama, p. 16 (rice); ZUMA Press, Inc./ Alamy, p. 18; titoOnz, p. 20 (flag); Sipa USA/ Alamy, p. 20 (Agnes Monica Muljoto); NaughtyNut, p. 21 (Borobudur Temple); B_BEUM, p. 21 (Kelimutu Crater Lakes); Danaan, p. 21 (Komodo National Park); audiovektor, p. 22.